DREAM BUILDER

THE STORY OF ARCHITECT PHILIP FREELON

by Kelly Starling Lyons

illustrated by Laura Freeman

afterword by Philip Freelon

Lee & Low Books Inc.
New York

VISION

In Phil Freelon's world, art breathes dreams to life.

Everywhere he looks around his Philadelphia home, paintings and drawings greet him from the walls. Phil listens to his parents discuss artists at the dinner table. He watches his big sister splatter canvases with creativity. He plays basketball with his buddies and carries a sketchbook around his neighborhood. Buildings, roses, people passing on the street: Phil sees them all and draws clear and strong.

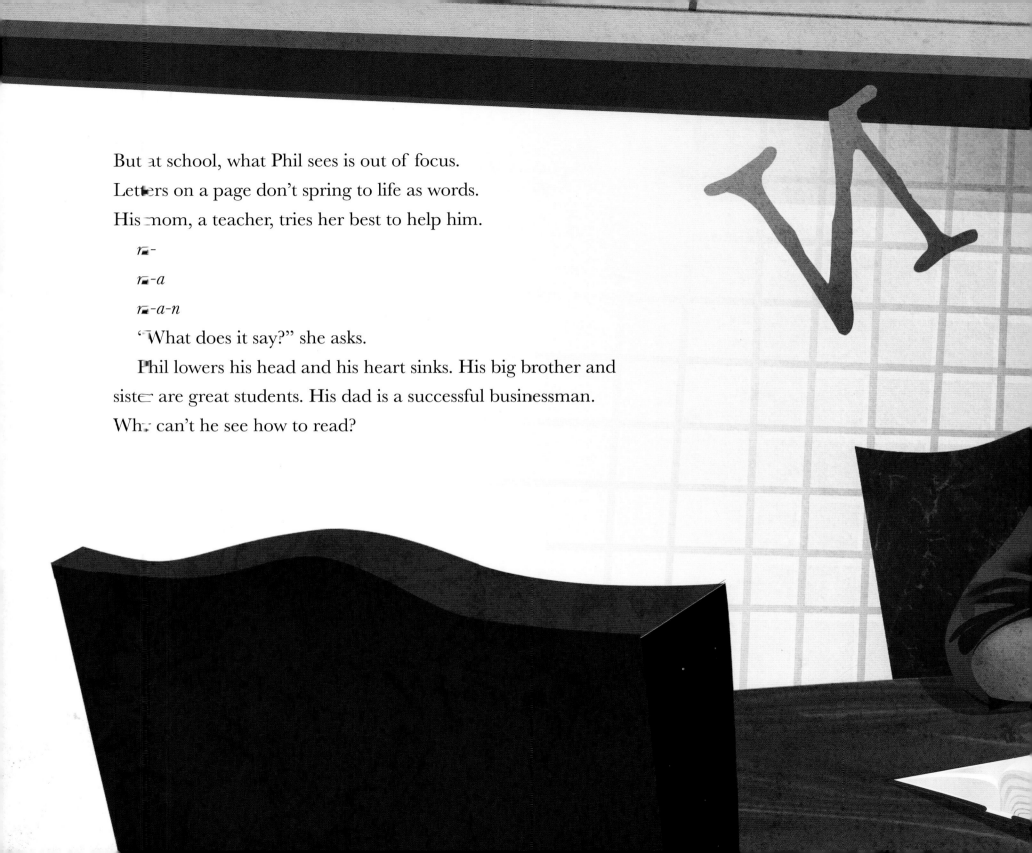

But at school, what Phil sees is out of focus.
Letters on a page don't spring to life as words.
His mom, a teacher, tries her best to help him.

r̄-

r̄-a

r̄-a-n

"What does it say?" she asks.

Phil lowers his head and his heart sinks. His big brother and sister are great students. His dad is a successful businessman. Why can't he see how to read?

Someone in his family shows him a strength he holds inside. His Pop Pop, Allan Randall Freelon, is an educator and Harlem Renaissance painter. In his studio, Phil sees pastel homes by harbors, fishermen. Still-wet canvases and palettes with oily colors dare him to touch.

One day the two of them walk through the woods. Phil darts this way and that until Pop Pop tells him to sit by his side on a log.

"Close your eyes and listen," Pop Pop says.

Phil hears birds crooning and squirrels scampering across crunchy leaves. He smells the fragrance of earth. He feels the breeze dance across his honey skin.

Phil is seeing the world with an artist's inner eye.

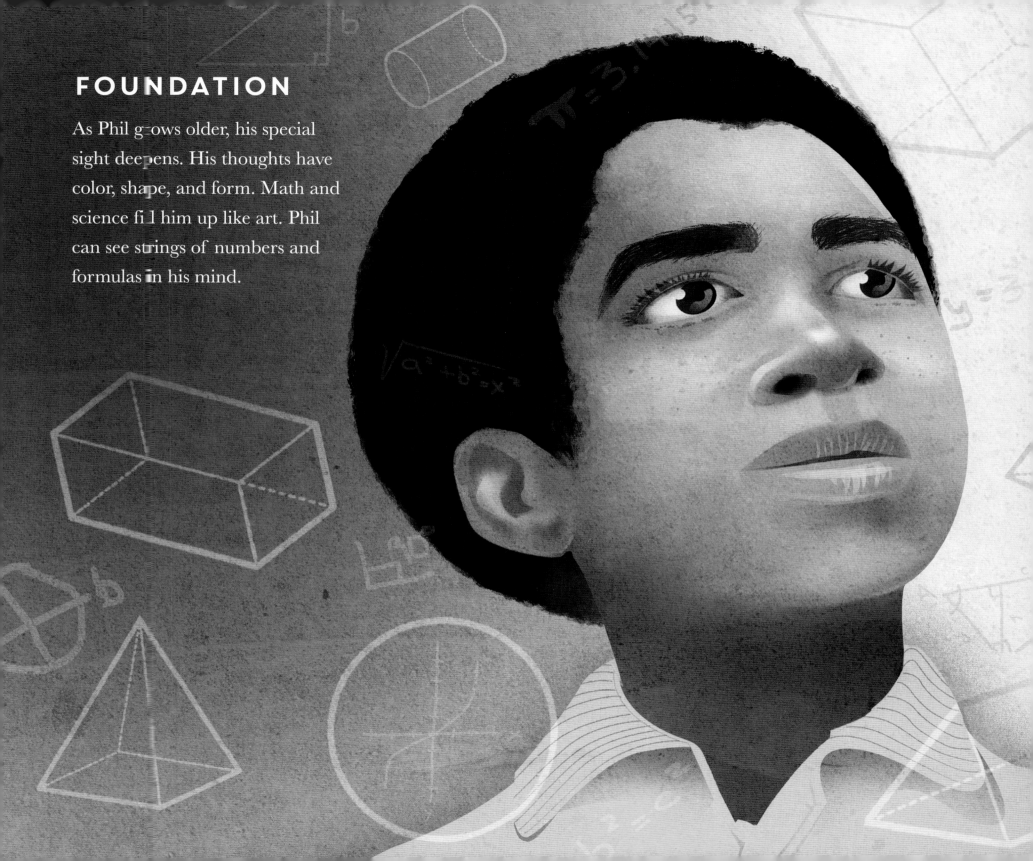

FOUNDATION

As Phil grows older, his special sight deepens. His thoughts have color, shape, and form. Math and science fill him up like art. Phil can see strings of numbers and formulas in his mind.

Reading takes longer to master. His mom and sister recite Shakespeare for fun, but Phil freezes when called to read aloud in class. He struggles to find joy in books until he realizes that words can create images too. In time, those story portraits show him new worlds just like art.

Phil explores different media. He doesn't just draw.
He writes essays and poems. He can see the shape of
a car inside a block of balsa wood. He builds, using
his senses to create. When his father gifts him models
after business trips, Phil spreads pieces of battleships,
cars, and planes out like a puzzle. He doesn't need
directions to know where each piece should go.

Soon his paintings, sculptures, and models begin
to reflect the times. He carves African masks from
bars of Ivory soap. *Black Is Beautiful. Say It Loud, I'm
Black and I'm Proud.* They're not just mottoes. They're
beliefs that live in him.

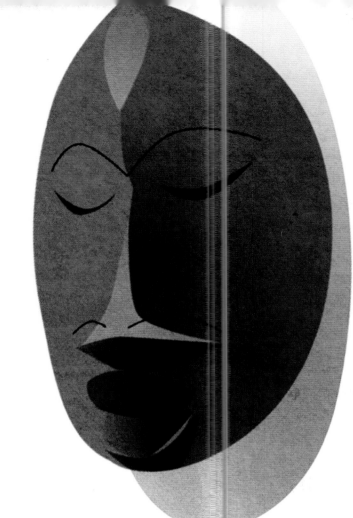

His father's stories are part of him too.

Stories of having to sleep in a different Southern hotel than his white colleagues.

Stories of being the only Black man in airports except for the porters.

Stories of being mistaken for an athlete instead of a businessman.

In his proud, Black neighborhood, Phil sees people who never make the news. His neighbors are doctors, suit-and-tie-wearing detectives, teachers, friends learning to play concert piano.

Phil hears a chorus around the nation shouting for justice and equality. When his father is at the March on Washington, Phil watches on TV and feels like he's there with his dad, soaking in Dr. King's dream.

FRAME

At Central High School, Phil signs up for a drafting class. When the teacher asks the students to look at the front of a machine and draw the other three sides, Phil gazes deep inside and can see what's out of view. He becomes the top student in his art and drafting classes. He wins industrial design competitions.

An idea emerges until it becomes clear as a snapshot. Phil wants to be an architect, someone who designs buildings. A perfect blend of his strengths in art, math, and science.

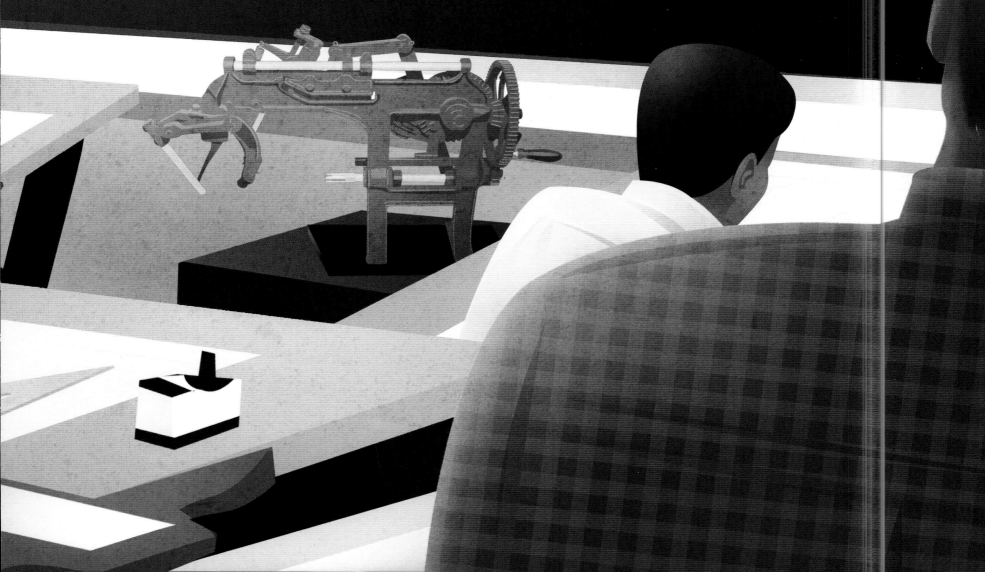

At Hampton University, a historically Black college, Phil aces every architecture lesson, tutoring classmates who need help. Later, when he attends North Carolina State University's School of Architecture, he soars too. But he wonders why they never study anything created by people who look like him.

On his own, he discovers Black architects who designed celebrity homes and a university chapel. He reads about African and Islamic builders his classes left out. He thinks about artists like his Pop Pop, whose work made unsung people and places seen.

One summer while Phil's still a student, he takes the lead in designing a solar greenhouse in Virginia. As the structure grows and glistens, a dream begins to take shape. Phil wants to make the world better through what he creates.

FORM

As an architect, Phil turns wishes into buildings, with doors and windows, plumbing and lights. By the time he founds his own firm in North Carolina, his mission is clear. He will not design prisons or casinos. Phil creates schools, libraries, bus stations, museums. Places that help people, that show everyday beauty, that celebrate heritage and fill hearts with joy.

TENLEY-FRIENDSHIP
NEIGHBORHOOD LIBRARY
WASHINGTON, DC

DURHAM STATION
TRANSPORTATION CENTER
DURHAM, NC

THE NATIONAL CENTER
FOR CIVIL AND HUMAN RIGHTS
ATLANTA, GA

CENTER FOR CIVIL AND HUMAN RIGHTS

REGINALD F. LEWIS MUSEUM OF MARYLAND
AFRICAN AMERICAN HISTORY & CULTURE
BALTIMORE, MD

Then one day Phil hears about a dream imagined decades before he was born.

In 1915, fifty years after the end of the Civil War, people dreamed of a national memorial to honor Black soldiers and sailors. That dream grew until they could see a museum that would rise like a phoenix on the Washington Mall.

A museum to honor Black achievement.

A museum to show Black resilience, strength, and pride.

For decades, that dream was deferred.

But in 2003, a national commission makes it come true. A museum will be created that documents Black history, life, and culture. Phil and architects around the world want to design it.

DREAM

Years later, the commission chooses Phil and architect Max Bond to create the preliminary master plan. For months, they work together, making a guide to future spaces and exhibits. In 2008, an international competition is announced. The winning team will get to design and build the museum.

For this project, Phil and Max need a dream team. They want to include someone whose work is known beyond the United States. Phil and Max meet with David Adjaye, an acclaimed British Ghanaian architect. As the men talk, they watch one another's body language. Can they unite?

The team clicks. Phil will be lead architect, coordinating all aspects of the complex project. David will be lead designer, coming up with ideas in collaboration with the team. They have just sixty days to plan a dream passed down for generations.

They huddle around tables, talk on phones for
hours, send countless emails, and dig deep.

They look.

They see a structure shaped like a crown worn by African kings.

They see ironwork patterns forged by Black artisans.

They see a porch of welcome.

And they listen.

They hear the ocean, rocking ships of stolen people.

They hear footsteps marching for freedom and justice.

They hear voices of unsung heroes waiting for their day.

In front of the judges for the competition, Phil tells the story of the dream they want to build. He feels Pop Pop, his father and mother, his family with him. His models stand proudly. His word-pictures light up the room.

Soon, Phil hears the word that makes his heart sing: Yes! Their next mission is to get the museum open before Barack Obama, the first Black president, leaves office.

In 2016, a century after the dream was born, they deliver.

In the Contemplative Court, Phil reads
Dr. King's words: "until justice runs
down like water and righteousness like
a mighty stream." He closes his eyes
and smells the moisture of the falling
water, listens to the peaceful sound.
The museum rises near where his
father once stood as Dr. King shared
his dream. Phil thinks of Pop Pop, who
taught him to see like an artist; his
parents, who encouraged him to create
and imagine. He thinks of how every
experience led him to this moment.

Phil Freelon, the kid artist from
Philly, has become a builder of dreams.

WE ARE DETERMINED ... TO WORK AND FIGHT UNTIL JUSTICE RUNS DOWN LIKE WATER AND RIGHTEOUSNESS LIKE A MIGHTY STREAM.

MARTIN LUTHER KING JR 1955

AFTERWORD

Growing up, I didn't know any architects. I was drawn to the arts, and the talent that I displayed as a child was encouraged and nurtured by my family. When I discovered architecture in high school, I realized that art and creativity could be used to create buildings. Over time, I learned about the achievements of African American architects, including Julian Abele and Paul Revere Williams. I was inspired.

Coming of age during the height of the civil rights movement, I felt compelled to contribute in some way to the struggle for social justice. As my career as an architect evolved, I continually sought opportunities to bring my design skills into alignment with my desire to make positive contributions to my community and beyond. With many developmental steps along the way, these parallel aspirations ultimately led to my role as Architect of Record for the National Museum of African American History and Culture.

My involvement with this amazing project was an honor and a privilege—and the pinnacle of my career. The decades-long journey leading up to the museum's opening included significant contributions from countless individuals and organizations. While the architects portrayed in *Dream Builder* represent the leadership of the design team, it was Lonnie Bunch, the museum's founding director and now the secretary of the Smithsonian Institution, who was the driving force behind the realization of this new national landmark.

Clockwise from center: Phil Freelon; his daughter, Maya; his wife, Nnenna; and his sons, Pierce and Deen.

A special thanks goes out to Kelly Starling Lyons, who conceived of the idea for *Dream Builder* and wrote the story, and to Laura Freeman for her lovely illustrations. I also want to thank my wife, Nnenna Freelon, for her love and support over the years.

—Philip G. Freelon
May 31, 2019

AUTHOR'S NOTE

When I moved to North Carolina more than a decade ago, I heard about the Freelon Group, a Black-owned architectural firm. Over the years, its influence seemed to be everywhere I went—the Durham Bulls Athletic Park, a terminal and parking garage at Raleigh-Durham International Airport, the Gantt Center in Charlotte, the Reginald F. Lewis Museum in Baltimore. I was proud and intrigued.

As I learned more about the founder, Phil Freelon, I realized that along with creating important spaces, Phil built hopes and dreams. He was a founding member of the Triangle East Chapter of 100 Black Men, which focuses on uplifting and empowering youth. He worked with the Harvard Graduate School of Design and the architectural firm Perkins + Will (where he was design director of the North Carolina practice) to establish the Phil Freelon Fellowship Fund. He taught at his alma maters, North Carolina State and M.I.T., and mentored people who wanted to follow his path.

Then I read about Phil's work as the lead architect for the National Museum of African American History and Culture (NMAAHC). I was there on the NMAAHC's opening day with my husband, children, and friends. Gazing at that bronze crown on the National Mall made us feel like kings and queens. The exhibits moved and amazed us, but we were caught in the museum's spell before we walked in the door. People had already suggested I write a picture book about Phil. Visiting the museum made me want to write one even more.

A couple years ago, I got my chance. My agent let me know that an editor at Lee & Low Books was interested in publishing a story about an architect who designed the NMAAHC. I immediately suggested Phil. When I reached out to him, Phil graciously responded that he was happy to participate in the project, seeing it as a way to inspire more kids of color to consider architecture as a career.

Over a series of meetings, I interviewed him and his wonderful wife, Grammy-nominated jazz singer and composer Nnenna Freelon, in their home. Slowly, a story began to take shape of a young artist who found his calling and used it to honor Black contributions and culture. Phil was proud of his partnership with Sir David Adjaye, the museum's lead designer, and architectural pioneer J. Max Bond Jr. who died in 2009. I asked Phil how it felt to be the NMAAHC's lead architect.

"It was a dream," he said. "The commission of a lifetime."

With every project, Phil showed all of us how to dream bigger and bolder. He was a man of integrity, talent, and vision. I mourned with people around the nation when Phil passed away in July 2019 from amyotrophic lateral sclerosis (ALS). His brilliant legacy lives on in his wife, Nnenna; in his children, Deen, Pierce, and Maya, and his grands; in the stunning museums and spaces he designed; and in everyone he touched. This book is a tribute to Phil and all of the dream builders around the world.

I'm so honored that Phil and Nnenna entrusted me with his story. Thank you to both of them for opening their home and hearts. Thank you to my agent Caryn Wiseman, editor Cheryl Klein, the Lee & Low family, and illustrator Laura Freeman; Carole Boston Weatherford; Bridgette A. Lacy; Judy Allen Dodson, Shelia Reich, Susan Taylor, and Dominique Brown; and my husband and children, always.

The next time you pass or read about something Phil created, think about the incredible man who made it. He was once a kid just like you with a big heart and big dreams. You can be a dream builder too. Believe in yourself, work hard, and use your gifts to help our world gleam.

—Kelly Starling Lyons
August 1, 2019

BIBLIOGRAPHY

This manuscript is based on extensive interviews with Philip and Nnenna Freelon as well as the following resources:

Bolden, Tonya. *How to Build a Museum: Smithsonian's National Museum of African American History and Culture.* New York: Viking Books for Young Readers, 2016.

Eanes, Zachary. "Phil Freelon Steps Down as Managing Director of Perkins + Will's NC Practice." *News & Observer*, May 11, 2017.

Gunts, Edward. "Two Men, One Vision." *Baltimore Sun*, June 5, 2005.

Lacy, Bridgette A. "Durham Architect Phil Freelon Building on the African American Tradition." *North Carolina Arts Council*, June 27, 2011.

National Archives Foundation. "National Archives Museum Welcomes African American Museum with Display." Posted September 22, 2016. https://www.archives.gov/press/press-releases/2016/nr16-94/.

National Museum of African American History and Culture. "A Century in the Making: The Journey to Build a National Museum." Posted August 24, 2016. https://nmaahc.tumblr.com/post/149430396115/a-century-in-the-making-the-journey-to-build-a/.

———. https://nmaahc.si.edu.

Saunders, Chris. "Transformational Alumni: From NC State to the Smithsonian, Phil Freelon is an architect with stories to tell." *NC State Magazine.* https://www.ncsu.edu/transformational-alumni/freelon/.

Waggoner, Martha, with contributions by Allen G. Breed and Mike Householder. "Architect shapes nation's view of African American history." *Chicago Sun-Times*, February 14, 2017.

Welton, J. Michael. "Master Builder: Phil Freelon." *Walter*, June 1, 2017.

———. "Philip Freelon, Lead Architect of the Smithsonian's African American Museum." *Washington Post*, February 18, 2012.

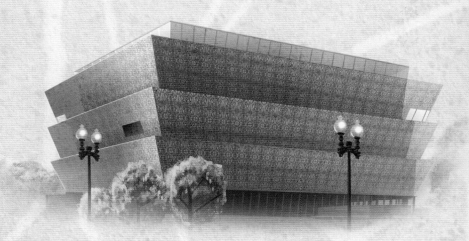

For Phil and Nnenna Freelon and their beautiful family, with love and gratitude. And for my friend, architect ElDanté C. Winston. — K.S.L.

To my parents, Jim and Trudy, who taught me through their actions what dedication and bravery looked like . . . and who always, always encouraged me and believed in me. Missing you, Mom and Dad! — L.F.

Text copyright © 2020 by Kelly Starling Lyons
Illustrations copyright © 2020 by Laura Freeman
Afterword copyright © 2020 by the estate of Philip G. Freelon
Photo credits: Phil Freelon, 1970s © the estate of Philip G. Freelon; family photo © 2018 by Lissa Gotwals; NMAAHC photo © 2016 by Noah Willman. All used with permission.

Edited by Cheryl Klein | Designed by Ashley Halsey
Book production by The Kids at Our House
The text is set in Baskerville with the display font in Core Circus
The illustrations were created using Photoshop

Manufactured in China by Toppan
10 9 8 7 6 5 4 3 2 1
First Edition

Library of Congress Cataloging-in-Publication Data
Names: Lyons, Kelly Starling, author. | Freeman, Laura (Illustrator), illustrator.
Title: Dream builder : the story of architect Philip Freelon / by Kelly Starling Lyons ; illustrated by Laura Freeman.
Description: First edition. | New York : Lee & Low Books Inc., [2020] | Includes bibliographical references. | Audience: Ages 6-8 | Audience: Grades 2-3 | Summary: "A biography of Philip Freelon, whose rich family history and deep understanding of Black culture brought him to the role of lead architect for the Smithsonian's National Museum of African American History and Culture"— Provided by publisher.
Identifiers: LCCN 2019028043 | ISBN 9781620149553 (hardcover)
Subjects: LCSH: Freelon, Philip G.—Juvenile literature. | Architects—United States--Biography—Juvenile literature. | African American architects—Biography—Juvenile literature.
Classification: LCC NA737.F735 L96 2020 | DDC 720.92/2 [B]—dc23
LC record available at https://lccn.loc.gov/2019028043